DARK ANIMALS

Wild Pressed Young Poets' Anthology 2019

Wild Pressed Books

First Edition

ISBN 978-1-9164896-6-0

DARK ANIMALS ©2019 by Wild Pressed Books.
Copyright for individual poems remains with the authors.

Cover Design by Tracey Scott-Townsend

Published by Wild Pressed Books: 2019
Wild Pressed Books, UK Business Reg. No. 09550738
http://www.wildpressedbooks.com
All Rights Reserved.

No part of this publication may be reproduced or transmitted in any form by any means electronic, mechanical, photocopying, recording or otherwise, without the prior permission of the copyright owner.

The publisher has no control over, and is not responsible for, any third party websites or their contents.

To the Young,

hold on, and hope.

DARK ANIMALS

List of Authors and their Poems

Luke Cable   Black Magic
                      Hurts
                      Next Time

Keilan Colville   A Derelict Cottage on the Knocks Road
                      Acceptance
                      Living the Kübler-Ross Model

Luca Goaten   Dreamland
                      i
                      Weapon-Take

Andrew Gooch   Carnal Excuses
                      Get It
                      Psychosis Whispers

Elen Griffiths   Partridge and Pear
                      Records
                      Solva, Sisters

April Hill   Bad Water
                      Seamstress
                      Tuna

Rebecca Kane   Meltdown
                      Swimming Pool 2007
                      The New God

Arun Kapur   Dove
                      Rich
                      Seize

Sian Mitchell   Notre Dame
                      The Pilgrim's Way

Vaishnavi Parihar	This Little Piggy
	Ode to the Sea
Lauren Ranson	On Achieving
	Trees
Nia Wyn Roberts	Out of the House
	Welsh Not
	Working Girls
Grace Royal	I
	Red Velvet Tomorrow
Natasha Rubins	Customs
	Rose Water
Hester Ullyart	Summer in England, 2019
	Where Sleeping Giants Lie
	Your Dark Animal

Contents

Living the Kübler-Ross Model 1
Summer in England, 2019 4
Weapon-Take 7
Next Time 8
A Derelict Cottage on the
    Knocks Road 10
Ode to the sea 12
Acceptance 14
Carnal Excuses 15
Seamstress 16
Seize 17
i 18
Solva, Sisters 19
Bad Water 22
Records 24
This Little Piggy 26
Meltdown 28
Dove 29
Dreamland 30
Black Magic 32
Notre Dame 34
Red Velvet Tomorrow 36
The New God 39
Welsh Not 40
On Achieving 42
Get it 43

The Pilgrim's Way
    written in response to the Worcester Pilgrim 44
Where Sleeping Giants Lie 45
I 46
Customs 48
Swimming Pool, 2007 50
Out of the House 51
Hurts 52
Trees 53
Rich 54
Rose Water 55
Tuna 56
Partridge and Pear 57
Psychosis Whispers 58
Working Girls 59
Your Dark Animal 60

Living the Kübler-Ross Model

    My room looks so white today.
After soothing crashes of August rain
have flooded the cul-de-sac with grey
the reluctant skies have opened, are limp
        and lame. They told me not to waste the day
        but it seems that instead
        the day has wasted me.

        I too am limp and lame
        remembering
        the past pain.

I will never understand them.
these days
That bring with them
the lacklustre stream
of death memories
as if they came directly
from a hypodermic needle
into the blood.

Days where the whiteness of cloud
and the greyness of empty roads blot
recalling the lengthy hospital corridors.
Days where the wind slips between the
window imitating failing lungs.
Days where I become so overwrought
in the past that my muscles jitter
with restless mortality
and ask me to leave the
limbo of the empty house
and walk into the
murmuring winds.

And sometimes I do.

The growing rustle of tall old trees
and the brief flashes of light
call upon the opening of my mind
to let the free gales
of cold air
clasp onto my memories
and whisper to them.

What they are saying?
I don't know
but afterwards I feel the
rush of their wailing flow.
they are free to come and
they are free to go.

When they come I
collapse and let the thunder
pelt my delicate psyche
      with the image of a burial
      the sound of halted breath
      and the thought of a mind
now limp and lame.

      But when they go
I lift my frame
from the grey and gritty murk of depression
      and just keep walking
because
it is only outside in the cold
in the tempest where I can
confront the storm itself

not inside
where I hide low moods
under blue bed duvets.

When I come back
and sit down

I know that I
was right.

> These days will come and go
> because it is all they can do.
> All I have to do is let them know
> that they don't last forever.

Keilan Colville

Summer in England, 2019

The weather in this never ending May
threatens – like a siren to a ship.

Air's thick, full, clammy,
stick-slips off under brief rains.

The clay wind holds it's thumb to the wing of the windmill
      by the front door.
That thing cost me five British pounds from a budget store
Made in China –
Cheap wings pivot joy against damp bricks.

We push through the wet green hedge, clunk the gate shut.
Our secret garden, leading out to lampposts and graffiti.
Dodge the dog crap and heavy nettles, on a street
where once were thorn bushes for Princes to hack down,
a broken white wing-mirrored car spreading bonnet wide
gets covered in a crow's mess.

Here, now, the wild flowers grow as dandelions,
Past's grunting pigs all replaced by ducks,
ruffled feathers settling in cracks where tree roots split the
      tarmac.
Old Tomcat's eyes laze still, gazing at the steam, moss on
      plastic,
water evaporates on his upturned bin lid throne.

And way above us all, an old sun, silent, roaring behind the
      haze.
Squint. Shield your eyes from its walled glare.
Badum–badum– two girls with Eastern foreign vowels
blade by in short shorts emblazoned with the brand of
      Primani.

Paving stones clunk a universal language
I am fifteen. I am fifteen. I am fifteen.

Get in the car.
Pump up the petrol – unleaded – watch the British digits roll high on a screen 'til it clicks.
Black fuel drips on the concrete, fast smell of childhood, sitting in the booster seat.
Cue behind a woman with a Subway lunch – processed meat wrapped in cling wrap.
The lady behind the counter jumps out of her skin
You are the spit of your mother!
Time recoils, time repeats.

Drive out. Trawl the lines of old roads, new,
green fields, past factory skylines, few.

The world is a flat rippled dome,
a table-spread with flower heads- yellow, dark green,
a sheet of lime velvet, stroked by a breeze.
Below the waves rock – tectonic plates groan with the weight.

This Island is uneasy.
Can you hear it creak?

Monuments to times gone by mark the skyline.
A concrete curve, black and white industries fading to grey,
chimneys, climbing frames towering up to clouds of man-made gas.

The Gods who once used us for play are stonewalling us.
Metal ladders cut mid-sky, high rungs to nowhere.
Somewhere in the graveyard by the paint shop we passed
Jack's beanstalk lies, it's thick root heavy, vine gone to seed.

At our destination
a castle stands, once it framed a draw bridge to the ocean
but the pier is long gone.

Just the sea. Windmills churn on the horizon.
We clamber to the boulders, our journey stopped at the breakers edge.

Large rocks protect the shoreline.
Long before we were born,
the hands of a Giant dropped them like crumbs from his
    pocket.

I want to go further, but there is no fleet to collect us,
so we stay.

There – can you hear it? Somewhere in the distance,
I think –
a dragon blows fire, wings beat.
The public statue quakes in its foundation by the council
    pond.

Look closely – do you see?
That dot on the horizon, it's getting closer.

Hester Ullyart

Weapon-Take

I imagine they landed in this mud
like lightning: a roar, a cry,
saltwater spray wild in their eyes,
their boots sinking into the wetlands.

Meanwhile I stand on the riverbank and watch
the culmination of the inlet veins
purring through the undergrowth
like the tenfoots through the terraces;

my snaking Humber, sighing out to sea.
Sunken, its mouth hung open
like a python processing prey
as the tide heaves along the riverbed.

I want to trace this water back.
Chase it up to the moors.
Rediscover the source, the start,
the centre of the fingerprint –

when I dig down through my words
I unroot bones –
Myton, Wyke, Holderness, Hull –
the remnants are on my tongue.

Like the bottom of a boat
breaching the water's surface,
a full dome of diaphragm
speaking to the nursery depths,

I enter an underworld of England:
brandished swords rattling against the sky,
a king witnessing cold wilderness,
madmen dancing around a pyre.

Luca Goaten

Next Time

Next time I fall in love,
I hope he will wield words of kindness
Like his mouth is the gate to heaven,
And God will hide us under her tongue;
I am the hollow of a skinless drum
And you are made of leather.

Next time I fall in love,
The word 'love' will be forbidden.
Don't say it, don't say it, *don't ever say it*
If you do not mean it.
Next time I fall in love,
He will take my soul and clean it.
Next time I kiss it will be for more than thrills
Love is a rapture; my sins will stand still.

Next time I fall,
It *will* be love; never again my window,
Or a hospital bed. Never again will I chase shadows
Around the halls of my head.
Next time I kiss
His eyes will be pools of cherry pink
The same colour as my fingertips;
He will lick around the wounds of my already bitten lips
And although I once thought myself rotten
He will take me in sweet sips.

Next time I fall in love,
It will be bliss.
I will find his heart buried in his kiss.
This is what I've waited for,
A love simple and plain.
No need for bruises
Or a ball and chain.
Love does not have to be a fool's game.

And if he does not love me back
My heart will beat all the same.

Next time I fall in love,
I will burn through my regrets
Like yellow-fingered cigarettes.
Yes, I love a man I have not yet met.

Luke Cable

A Derelict Cottage on the Knocks Road

I had taken that mountain road before –
Before I was pattering along and
Remembering young car journeys to my
Aunt's house that was nested firm in the hills.
Oh, how I looked forward to that swift drive
Which led to cups of tea and a chit-chat;
Though I was young then – in child's mania –
Missing the quiet, minute exchanges
Of hardship that plagued the adult landscape.
What it was to merely be; to exist.

When I was older, I revisited
That slant, meandering path of the past
By foot, where I saw much more than my youth –
The view of hometown in milky morning,
The pools of roadside reflection, littered
Down the lanes – 'til then I met a cracked ruin,
Devoured by roots that plunged into soil.
It looked as if the vines were to swallow
The building whole, with crumbling memory
Echoing in its forgotten presence.

It was a solemn place of decades gone
That I had passed by all my life, like the
Dead that lie in silent bogs waiting on
Loved ones to finally lay them to rest –
This lost home was now a purgatory
Of abstraction, as if it hadn't been
Material until my arrival.
Dawn was young, with a silky grey skyline
That dripped watercolour to ground, and I,
Having to take shelter, gazed to the dark

Interior, that was vacant to eyes.

I ripped through Nature's fingers and stepped in,
Finding a hull that chilled my skin and lungs
While my eyes focused to a slice of light
That protruded from overgrown windows.
Inside, it was impossible to think
That someone lived here, once, many years by –
My steps reverberated nothingness.
I sat awhile on a mangled staircase
In a mind-vacuum, void of thought or will

And as the cold grew on my cheeks and hands,
I realised that Time had forgotten
Me – the rain had ceased, the Church Bell rang out,
As if to tempt me out of this place.
I brought myself back in mind and comfort –
I left the way I went in, knowing well,
Though, that I had a warm haven waiting,
And it wouldn't be so eternally.
I had taken that mountain road before,
But Time treaded too, and showed me much more.

Keilan Colville

Ode to the sea

Gasping and quivering
I sprint to the seas,
Floating up and down
the alleys.

Breakdowns at one,
Mending by three.
The waves roll up
rocking me to sleep.

"Too much has happened
and I cannot breathe,
Eyes out there shooting rejection
I cannot see!"

I weep.

"So O! water –
if I jump,
Please let me sink.
I've had enough of this world
And I do not wish to swim."

Choking out words
from debris,
I speak.
An ichor fills my chest,
I weep.

The water,
The sea,
still pays no heed.
Just keeps humming under its breath
a deep melancholy,
"O! my dear child I cannot take you in,
Survival is the word.

And Survive you will.
Tonight, you may be drowning but you're not dying,
so please.
Do not give up on life without even trying."

Vaishnavi Parihar

Acceptance

I know all too well the difficulty
Of enduring a heavy brain –
To hold a waterlogged mind and still
Keep your head above your shoulders
As the world breathes down your shivering neck
Like a racing tidal weapon.
And you will want to resist with your might,
To tear the wave before it floods
Your head, but it will best you if you fight,
So you must let it hit you and
Submerge you – let yourself see the true depths;
The unstoppable world forces.
You will sink, but then beam from the sea-floor,
And find yourself floating in the
Bright silence of another day.

Keilan Colville

Carnal Excuses

You always stop once a phone rings.
You always stop once a friend knocks on the door.
You always stop once a stranger wanders by.
You always stop once I mention the wrong name.
You always stop once I admit a lie.
You always stop once I moan too loud.
You always stop once glass gets shattered.
You always stop once Netflix gets interesting.
You always stop once a taxi pulls up.
You always stop once you get bored.
You always stop once you realise you're being missed.
You always stop once you feel no fun.
I stop once you leave the next day.

Andrew Gooch

Seamstress

Thread in a needle,
I move. Through metal,
passed like a parcel between
each thumb-pad, skin cradle.
You always know the angle.

But I move through. Greece
conquered Rome. Woven
tight enough to hold. Dance
is the best bind, momentum the glue
that keeps you on your bicycle.

Thread in a needle, I grow
serpentine, shedding each hole.
Where is Eve? Where is the Apple?
Without me, there is no fable.
Without fruit, there are no vegetables.
Harvest-time, but you don't want to sow.
Without thread, there are no clothes.

April Hill

Seize

Sometimes it will take it's toll
Waking up, sucked-out soul.
Simple tasks seem to much to ask.
Wake up, put on a face and face up,
Open yourself and let the light in,
Open yourself and let the day in.
Doubt is a cloud that will come and go,
Taking you high and all the way low,
It can lay you down, back on your knees.

Rise, this life is yours to seize.

Arun Kapur

i

I am a murder of crows. I am the dull moon
that waits for nighttime.

I am the sound of rainfall.

I am four days submerged in June
lifting my face to the wet sky.

I am solar panels

beneath the wringing-out of clouds:
I am Revelations tacked onto roof tiles.

I am gravity-slicked in a downpour.

A heavy black coat
grounded in the earth.

I am the emptiness in the day.

A Tiber in the grass.
A cup of tea left by the kettle.

I am forgotten warmth; I am lower than the leaves.

Luca Goaten

Solva, Sisters

I

July, 1908. Solva. West Wales.
Boats in the harbour bobbed and stayed.
The wheel on the woollen mill turned
quick as a seamstress' hand, steady as her gaze.
Miss Kenney paced the makeshift stage.

On tip-toe, the whole town:
fishwives and lime girls straining to catch sight
of the English suffragette. O Miss Kenney saw it all:
how the women bobbed from one calloused foot
to the other, heads raised, on their arms how the hair

raised to goosepimples. Cut against the sea's spray
her voice rose with purpose, eyes all ablaze.
"Votes for all. Vote down this government. Brothers
and Sisters of Solva, lend an ear to the women's cause!"

The women were listening, but the men were having none of
    it.
*That jumped-up Suffragette. Little slut. Who the hell does
    she–*
They threw fruit and jeered. One man came up behind,
smeared gooseberry against Miss Kenney's cheek,
while the others cheered.

Afterwards, they'd said she was an English whore.

II

Heave the mill's wheel forward to December 1918. It was
    Miss Kenney's time.
Those men were dead. Those Solva sisters, workers at the
    lime
kilns, fishwives and washerwomen, or some of them, folded
    their slips
and shaking placed them in the ballot box, for the first time.
One wrote to her, enclosed a news clipping: of women

voting. In a General Election. Suffrage sublime.

III

Heave the mill's wheel once more, to December 2018. By the
    lime
kilns, we chance to find her signature, *"A Kenney. 1908"*,
and a clipping of her Solva visit in the Pembroke Times.
We try not to laugh at the account: how the woman
    revolutionary
is turned Charlie Chaplin on stage, pelted with gooseberries.

Now, we are everything Miss Kenney had in mind:
You all tiger mother, warrior-wombed,
me, tiger-cub daughter, mouth all motor. The same age
as Annie Kenney was in Solva,
but all the things she couldn't be,

back then: a solicitor, constituent, voter.
We walk the cliff path, and talk of
Michelle Obama's recent memoirs,
of how she fought the White House from within –
not once letting that man's world pass her by.
To crass men's slurs, her enviable reply:

"When they go low, we go high"
We say it in unison on the cliff path -
Mother, daughter – and I catch your eye.
Long before Michelle became First Lady, you taught me
that when women's voices are at stake,

we take the fight to the sky.

Elen Griffiths

Bad Water

What did you want from me?

Did I imagine you? All blue,
electric icicle, water that is not
clear. A dream
that begins with fish, shoals of them
raining in, yellow and tropical even though
we are in Glasgow. A dream
with exaggerated fins. A dream
that clings

like wet clothing to skin.
I am not yours to observe.
Understanding is not
undressing, and I am not
standing over you in your living room until
I am standing over you in your living room.
You predict lovers like a weather forecast.
Bad water. You open your mouth
and it tastes too warm and sweet
to not be from concentrate.
You wring clouds with both hands,
try to juice fruit from trees
you did not seed. Did not feed.
A late father is not a father.
A witness is not intimate

and this is not first person.
You only saw what two eyes
can see, but I felt their body
with every nerve ending. Know this:
even mothers don't own their fetuses.

We fuck up into
the possibility, and bility, and ility,
and no one holds us after. No one says
you were too rough. No one says
you were too gentle.

April Hill

Records

When you ring the plastic doorbell
and appear with *News to Nowhere* at the
entrance to my flat well I can hardly believe it

from Miss Havisham
to Maid Marion I have my pick of leading ladies
after which to fashion myself

but your eyes make me Jane Morris, almost

not quite a flower of the mountain
someone said I was studiedly difficult once a daughter
        of the smogged up city   or some mad girl
    laughing in a shawl

in the living room you play records of
Irish protest songs and we dance
around the Persian rug   mesmerised each time the
    needle

hits the vinyl   you can be who you want here I said
the fragmented self replenished
on cracked phone screens we swap

whatsapp signs of hearts and
butterflies our eyes feasting on each other
in the kitchen *eating bread and butter*

like it's ostrich and cobra wine. [1]
O who knows who I am
when you hold me in your Ulsterman hands

under the cherry tree by the formica table
and your eyes are salt-of-the-moon socialist,
your hair like dark sunshine

[1] © Father John Misty, Chateau Lobby #4 (in C for two virgins)

and my pulse ticks wildly like a revolution
of the vinyl against the needle, and your mouth
opens against mine like some antediluvian

notion of the divine O
world without time

Elen Griffiths

This Little Piggy

In my smile you can decipher things unrelated,
like the scavenger that was you,
nibbling on my heart,
crusading and cutting through my veins,
petting and building a home
inside me first,
and then filling my organs
with rosemary and sage.

Setting my insides on fire
and then leaving me in ashes,
You smiled,
Unable to decipher my pain.
And, oh I wish I could elucidate the pain,
the exquisite pain of knowing,
how much I cared,
But no, you don't
and maybe you never actually cared.

So what
If I'm just a piggy?
It's you who brought me up
like your own baby
and then secured my cuffs
to bricks
so that you could drown me
with the waves.

But now, as I swim here in this ocean
Of blood,
Can't you see
the wicked little world
You've created?
The deluded fantasy
That keeps you

Fascinated?
Kicking me out
Bathing me in water
stripping me of my leather skin
and then putting me in a cage?
Isn't it all just too inhumane?

An ocean nevertheless, of
Water replaced by blood,
Love replaced by labour,
Skin replaced by leather
And brains replaced by pumpkins.
Oppression and violence, a few overused words,
I deal with it every day.

Yet I hope,
my snorts reach you as a poem,
and cries touch you in some levitated frame,
Someday.
To protect me and mine from a world,
full of odious vermin
where every
today begins with a eulogy;
and tomorrow ends in a sermon.

Vaishnavi Parihar

Meltdown

I stir and swallow the bitter acid
Nuclear and damp.
A fever bitting at my lips,
Screams crushed with sharpened teeth,
A pulsing blue
Electric,
Behind the eyes –
Poison has a new face
White and cold,
An ignorant light
That won't realise the dark is here.
I will show it the night,
Suffocate it in sour light,
Crave this burn inside me.
A motionless
Motion,
A need to yell
With a tongue ripped out
No friends here,
Nothing but burning.

Rebecca Kane

Dove

Grey skies, clouds above the sea.
No love is stronger.
You left me tranced within your gaze,
I am now stronger.

I soar like a dove.

Arun Kapur

Dreamland

My nan and granddad often took me to the seaside
as a child. We would drive there –
stopping on the way in a lay-by

to sit in silence, eat sandwiches,
drink tea from a flask,
watch the electricity pylons

concertina off into the distance
strung together by their wires
as if holding hands across the hills.

And then when we arrived we would just walk
up and down and again: the seafront:
weathered by wind, abandoned

to the tides, each time it was the same,
as though we had all been there forever,
and the wrinkles sunk further into their faces

while I watched and they stared
out, withstanding the horizon,
waiting among the grey for the evening.

(On the beach the waves break white like eggshells
and a few dogs swim out in the sea, leaving
only their wet heads visible like seals

and their owners sink into the sand
and the drizzle
and the dark clouds gather

like the seagulls overhead.) So we would retreat
back to the amusements –
the neon machines and the no-joy coins –

and enter as a sign outside proclaimed
DREAMLAND WELCOMES YOU
but we would all be exhausted

and soon go for fish and chips instead.
Always the same place because *It's always been
the best, but it's a little worse now*, they'd mutter

before we would leave like everyone else.

Luca Goaten

Black Magic

I don't meditate, I self-medicate,
But you wouldn't know because you're always coming home late.
I text you on Saturday, but you replied on the Monday
I never knew love could handle this much hate.

When I first saw you, you cast a spell on me –
A spell you knew would never set me free.
A hex in your sex; you said you wanted me
But then I turned self-destructive,
Every night you're out hunting,
Find another boy, catch your breath and start grunting,
I know you're up to something,
You tell me that its nothing.
I've caught so many lies even your bluffs start bluffing.

I find pictures of your new boy and I create dolls with voodoo,
Nobody has seen me like this – nobody but you

And I keep trying black magic
Like a genie with a drug habit;
I look at love and know that I can never have it.
I just wanted to taste you and now I am an addict,
I've fucking had it. This lover's madness
Needs to end – if you really hate me, just call me friend.

I keep trying black magic, banish that boy.
I have another drink, slip myself into the void.
You pull me out every time and call me paranoid;
Tell that to the boys you can't seem to avoid.

You and him create black magic and I put magic in my blunts.
You called me insane, so I called you a cunt.
You play me like a game – just another fucking stunt.
He's loved you for a day – I've been here six months.

I keep trying black magic – you called me tragic –
You pull another boy out of your hat like a rabbit.

I keep trying black magic –
Like a genie with a drug habit;
I look at love and know that I will never have it.

Luke Cable

Notre Dame

Her proud, majestic beauty
Is lit with a flickering flame.
Dancing in the water below
A leaping, sweeping, creeping glow
Begins her ancient stones to maime.

Across the bridge the cries begin
To shatter the peace around.
The shouts of shock, of awe and fear
That people cannot bear to hear,
A disbelieving, grieving sound.

Flames pierce the sky with orange tongues,
Clawing, pulling, tearing the night.
Centuries of sightless eyes
Gaze on above the shouts and cries
And watch the rising amber light.

Yet in amongst the calls of fright
There floats a very different sound.
A gentle, rising, hopeful song
Which moves the gathering crowd along
As it walks towards the sacred ground.

At Notre Dame the song peals up
And reaches far into the sky.
Amidst the roar of flame and fire
The statues up above the quire
Catch 'Ave Maria' drifting high.

And when the flames begin to fade,
A victory in a desperate fight,
None will forget that quiet refrain
Which let the hopes of all remain
At Notre Dame that night.

Sian Mitchell

Red Velvet Tomorrow

I dream in red velvet,
in cream dusted scarlet,
in shades of warm chocolate,
in the softness of flapjack.
I think of rich tomato
the stretch of mozzarella.
I dream of the pain au chocolat
and the peanut butter cheesecake.
I think of the untasted
with forlorn longing;
I think of the consumed
with a sharp sickness.
I dream and I want.
I wake and I think and I don't.
I wake and I walk.
I wake and I think.
I wake and I dream.
I wake and I see
red velvet in all
my comfort nightmares.
Bagel, granola,
yoghurt, banana,
cereal, soup, rice cake,
no bun, no cheese,
small, light please.
I dream in warm chocolate,
taste it in my mouth,
leave it behind the glass,
and go walking, walking,
running on the spot,
wearing bones down,
wearing muscles down,
filing self down,

keeping things in the lines,
keeping things in the bounds.
I dream of red velvet,
of barbeque sauce,
of chocolate digestives,
of macaroni.
I dream of cereal in heated milk,
of soft, warm cookies,
of sweet potato fries.
I dream and I say,
today, I will change,
and then I remember
how I am supposed to be
starving myself.
I say and then remember
how I have taken that hand
and slipped and
slipped and slipped so easily,
so willingly, so knowingly,
so self-aware.
I watch the numbers and
tick off the boxes on a list
of how to self-destruct.
I will change, I say,
I will mend,
I will try harder
and then I walk in circles
until my feet bleed.
I dream in cherry yoghurt,
in beans on toast and garlic bread.
I cut something else from the day
and think I'm doing better.
So I'm still losing and
I feel so guilty, so scared,
so scared to lose,
so scared to gain

So scared and this
is going to be so hard – all this
letting go.
How will I manage when
things go slipping from
my clasping fingers and
numbers pile up
and circles stop?
This is going to be so hard,
so hard it hurts my head.
I will mend,
I say.
I will change.
I will do this,
get through this.
Things have to change.
I say it and then I start
the circles and the numbers and
I dream in red velvet
and think,
tomorrow.
I'll have it
tomorrow.

Grace Royal

The New God

i erupt into the small room
filled to the brim with light
and drums screaming
sticking to everyone like sweet molasses
let me in
consume me
sticky oil coating every soul
I'm ecstatic
full of flavour
a burst of skin
that I let flow and break
off a piece of me like a
communion wafer
a toast of honey to the holy
scoop up the syrup
become the god you prayed for
a doppelgänger of the blessed
to be reborn
in smoke and
fear

Rebecca Kane

Welsh Not

We talk of persecution, day after day,
Children punished for where they were born,
The colour of their skin, the language that they speak,
The way they pray and mourn.

You always believe this happens,
In far off lands, Many years ago,
You would never believe that this could take place,
Close to home, A mere stones throw.

Nightmare inducing horror stories of caning,
For speaking your own language in your state school?
In your own country? With your own family?
Surely not, impossible, you say, not under British rule!

What is the point in speaking Welsh?
Everyone can speak English anyway.
It's a dying language, A dead language,
Non-developing language, English is the better way.

A plaque of wood, W.N.
Two letters caved onto the surface,
Carved into our history, the sting of medieval practices,
Beaten into our education system, doing my language a
    disservice.

"And we were singing,
Hymns and Arias,
Land of my fathers,
Ar hyd y nos."

And you tell me my language is dying,
As if it were my generations fault?
My language was beaten out of me long before I was born,
And you wonder why there was a revolt?

No, I am not to blame.

Nia Wyn Roberts

On Achieving

You don't expect
to be covered
head-to-toe
in pre-care tattoo cream.

Or for the feelings-anesthetist
to creep up on you at night,
stab you in the heart,
make off with a bag of your nerves,
and leave you in a buzzless void.

You don't envision
avoiding eye-contact with friends,
can't squeeze a smile
or pretend to be content.

No one ever said
your sense of thought
would be nothing,
no one ever whispered
you'd be numb.

Lauren Ranson

Get it

I don't watch films with Keanu Reeves in them.
I don't join in with the disdain for MP's.
I don't care for the way guitar strings feel on my fingers.
I don't want to share the name of my disorder.
I don't like sitting in the allocated safe space anymore.
But you don't get that, you don't get that, you just don't get that.

I don't understand the point of saying good morning every day.
I don't class wearing a nice shirt as a compliment.
I don't tell jokes but I'm still called 'funny'.
I don't look at people when they say hello to me.
I don't bother with invitations from tight-knit groups.
But you don't get that, you don't get that, you just don't get that.

I don't feel approved when others say nice things.
I don't know how it feels to live without anxiety.
I don't picture myself ever coming close to sex.
I don't walk alone just because it's exercise.
I don't cry when there's someone there to hug.
But you don't get that, you don't get that, you just won't ever get that.

Andrew Gooch

The Pilgrim's Way
written in response to the Worcester Pilgrim

Through vast lands
I leap, pray, and struggle.
The shadowy hills of home, the rushing river
All seize and fade within my mind
And I walk on.

The quiet peace of familiar fields, the still
Of mornings misty on the lake
And gentle chants which float
Over priory walls to bustling streets
Seem lost amongst the whirr of strange new worlds.

From sandy banks to salt-tossed seas,
Viridian fields, rich forests, craggy peaks,
I tread my way.
The dusty track ahead meanders
Through the sun-drenched valley.

My well-worn boots are not the first to tread this path,
Nor will they be the last.
Through icy nights and searing heat
I see my brothers fall, and falter,
And endure.

Endure, until at last we come
To the end of that great path.
Through dusty eyes I see the smiles which shine from those
    cracked faces
As they look upon the journey's end
And rest.

Sian Mitchell

Where Sleeping Giants Lie

The giant woke up with the apology.
Something rolled over,
something asleep.
Near a cave on a rock,
The hills shuddered and the grass shook

just a little
and the wind hushed the flowers under the tree.

Where I said goodbye to you,
you say hello to me.

Hester Ullyart

I

I hold the first self and it takes up my palm.
Its surface is smooth and reflective.
The shadows and lights and shapes of the world
echo and slide across its body –
the human body, painted abhumanly:
the human body, rounded, boneless,
and caught in primary colours.
Minute, delicate and simple.
It's large enough – too large perhaps –
and each eyelash can be seen, each
blank blue iris, each pupil.
It's divided into head and body,
simple, steady and sturdy.
Like the limpet, it cannot survive without its shell.

I open the self at the stomach
and a second self shows off its
stumpy eyelashes. It smiles
with a smudged mouth
that curls up to its streaming, rosy cheeks.
This one has been construed from five words,
chosen from a list of thirty.
The words are off-black
and blurred around the edges.
The lines cannot hold as they shrink.

With two turns of the second self, the third appears,
with its clipped wing lashes and unspeaking mouth.
It looks like a photo of myself
taken in a place I don't recognise
by a person I do not know.
It still has a head and a body.
The colours have not changed,
but the mouth cannot move now it's painted shut.

The final, unopening self is
shrunken, sprawling and splattered.
It speaks in colours and irregularities.
It slips through my fingers
and tries to stare up at me,
but the Unopening Self has no eyes.

Grace Royal

Customs

I was an extra in *Harry Potter and the Philosopher's Stone*.
Locked in the bathroom as the kids defeated the troll. 16
wondering if peeing would distract or add to the scene. I
befriended Ingrid
(the troll) over behind the scenes crusty muffins.
She was anxious about type casting
wondering if acting brainless and genderless is a step back.
I told her not to worry – but knew
the truth. The only way she would break America
would be sitting on it.
I was only able to be an extra through my Aunt
and her very good friend's next-door neighbour: Frances.
Frances always said I had a look about me.
Like I othered myself to tell a story that was only interesting
or painful to me.
Ingrid and I fooled around through *Chamber of Secrets*,
Prisoner of Azkaban and the first half of *Goblet of Fire*. At
that point the studio realised half the extras had crossed
over
into superfluous territory and dropping us meant they could
pay the main cast more.
Ingrid and I grew apart without the common thread.
I tried reaching out to her, but she was obsessed with the
idea of finding fame outside of Britain. Like being an other
in an othered location completed a secret inside of her.
One night in a lonely burst I texted: they won't accept you
there. I didn't even know what 'there' was –
picturing her outside a pub in the rain. She didn't reply and
I
deleted the message in shame. Years later, I saw her on a
poster for her dream role: *Lord of the Rings*
told from the perspective of the trolls. She was happy –
in the middle of a bright, gushing cast that were spilling over

each other in an effort to be loved by her. Wrapped in
armour as heavy and light as a body – accepted
without a need to declare
anything.

Natasha Rubins

Swimming Pool, 2007

I find the heavy feeling comes back as blunt as
A hammer to a skull
Sinking down
In a pool of blood
A soft drowning
Peaceful even.
No one really witnesses it
The murder
They float above it all,
Wishing me luck on my journey
With no destination
There is a foolish innocence to it
A paddling pool of thoughts
That seems to go deeper
And
Deeper
Until I am too embarrassed
To afraid to poke my head up
Again.
They'll laugh at me,
At the girl drowning
In the rubber pool with the yellow ducks
But I have kept them there
To bring comfort
But now they bring shame
As everything does.

Rebecca Kane

Out of the House

The bark, weathered silver,
Cracked, and blackened with damp.
Valleys of history,
Running through time.
Scent of earth and
Long remembered rain showers
Greys and browns,
Moss creeping from shadows
To bask in the rain.
A skirt of discarded leaves,
Yellow, Orange, littered with age spots,
Veins pumping life
To serrated edges,
Curling like paper
Burned for survival,
The October light,
Glistening like amber.
Roots straining,
Against centuries of dirt,
Meandering tracks beneath,
Pushing back progress, defiant.

And now? The gateway to home,
Solid. Square. Structured.
A passing resemblance,
Polished and varnished,
And smooth, untarnished,
Straight lines and inlay glass,
Glowing amber like the past.

Nia Wyn Roberts

Hurts

I keep trying black magic,
You're lying in your habits
But I still love you, god fucking damnit.

Luke Cable

Trees

Branches shake like alcoholic hands,
drop their skin to down another each September.

Tremble at the wind like police
caught them sipping the last thimble.

Sway intoxicated
at the slightest imbalance,
rooted in the street they grew up in.

Veins protruding sap pulse
like a cut on an artery line.

Cut down and daughter sowed
left their brothers to grow new friends,

grow more skin, start again.

Lauren Ranson

Rich

I don't create art to be rich,
I'm rich because I create art.
I don't express my vision for glory,
My vision is expressed to tell my story.
I don't seek limelight to be God-like,
My light guides me no matter how hard.
I don't seek power in false fans,
I power myself towards my plans.

Arun Kapur

Rose Water

I've been up all-night thinking about rose water and whether you're supposed to spray it or drink it or if there's some secret ethereal third meaning.

> Anne looks me in the throat and says, again, this time could be it.

I've been up all-night thinking about what makes rose and what makes water and

> she talks to me about the weather as I try to reassure her that it won't rain. Or maybe there's a chance, why not live in surprise? She talks to me about dosages, where it went wrong and

about which part – the rose or the water – needs to sacrifice itself for it to be whole.

> I call an ambulance so an adult can intervene and guide the high starred way.

I think about being the sky, rose-dipped and home to time.

> The hospital remembers us and when the nurse tells me to go home, I listen without moving. Picturing Anne's comments in the morning, her texts at night –

how it would feel to rain at will, to coat everyone like a thick layer of protective skin.

> I've been up all-night

Natasha Rubins

Tuna

You don't know
anything about me.
Fantasy, a word with
scales as slippery as a fish.
Pleasure that alliterates,
fabricates, separates
identity into silver speckled fins
and flippers that beat like racing
blood-meat. Underneath,
I am all sandwich-filling,
nothing you can keep
refrigerated. I said
when are you going to
take me up close and love me?

April Hill

Partridge and Pear

When you and I stood so
still next to our first evergreen
tree, all decked out in the corner,
I wanted to write you a carol. To do more

than merely mouth
turtledove and drummer boy, partridge and pear
tree, eyes all wonder, at you. But that night
there were no French hens

Nothing thronged in the air
outside our dilapidated flat
except the blue flash of police sirens, the roar of car horns,
the thud thud as the neighbour (like some sordid Saint Nick)

hauled his sack of Amazon
loot to the front door.
What can I say? This is London,
It's Christmas, I'm yours.

Elen Griffiths

Psychosis Whispers

Message from the subconscious.
These are the facts: I lost the game. They said never mind. I'm going home to bed.
Pass it on to the next voice along.

These are the facts: I was last in the game. They said things just to be kind. I'm going home to cry in bed.
Pass it on to the next voice along.

These are the facts: I was last because I am crap at games. They think I should have stayed home. I'm crying, wish I was dead.
Pass it on to the next voice along.

These are the facts: I came last because I am a piece of crap, everyone thinks I should stay out the way and leave them alone so I'm trying to end up dead
Pass it on to the next voice along.

These are the facts: I fail at everything I ever try because I am a piece of shit, everyone wants me to go away. I'm going to end up alone for the rest of my life, wish I was dead.
Pass it on to the brain.

These are the facts; I will always be alone, They all hate me, I'm going to kill myself.
Message received and understood.

Andrew Gooch

Working Girls

Perhaps you should look a bit more presentable?
Put some make up on your face?
Honestly, girls can be so emotional,
I only told you, you are a disgrace.

I think you should wear heels,
God your heels make such a loud noise,
On the hard kitchen floor.
Thank God! I thought you were going,
To tell me you were pregnant,
That would have been a kick out the door.

Thanks, you would make such a good secretary,
Honey, do this printing for me?

Another chocolate donut?
You need to take better care of yourself,
Sweetheart, you look amazing!
Have you lost some weight?

Should you be eating that?
Should you be saying that?
Should you be wearing that?
Darling, love, ducky, Bitch.

Wow, your boyfriend has a lot to put up with.

Nia Wyn Roberts

Your Dark Animal

A lot of people I know are sad at the moment.
Like the world has been tipped off its axis
just dipped a little off centre
huge and tiny movements, revolving on a distended tilt.

A multitude of why.
Seas in turmoil, ignorant mutterings of war,
cuts, anger, bleeding oil.

Gravity got a little heavier,
The sun a little further away.

But the bird on the wind-blown roof is still singing,
and I still love you.

Go to sleep in the darkness,
cover yourself in hope.
Surround yourself with the memory of those you've lost,
wait for the turn of Spring.

Death is a part of life.
I can see you – your dark animal, by a silent, still, pool at night
staring at the clear glass – your black eyes void and wide in its cool reflection.

Stay there all night in the dark grass. Stay until dawn.
Stay 'til your sad pupils turn from discs to pins.
Watch as life breaks through
like a mouth coming for air,
breaking the surface,
sending ripples to the dark corners.

While the world is tipped, the ants still gather their lost and carry them home,
and I still love you.

(Remember to look each other in the eye.
Hold on to touch. Be quick to laugh.)
And know that just under the cold earth,
lie seeds, planted before you were born,
patient, waiting for their time to break through the dirt,
huge and tiny, a million little pieces making up a world,
    bigger than you.

You are so beautiful.
You are every bit of this world. Just a little off kilter.
It'll come back around. It's just around the corner.
When you wake, the dog will still be barking behind the gate,
and I still love you.

Hester Ullyart

THE POETS

LUKE CABLE is a founding member of *No Larkin About* and represents queer spoken word in East Yorkshire. Luke is an eighteen-year-old non-binary poet who writes in depth about sexual assault, living with mental illness and the struggles of being young and queer.

KEILAN COLVILLE is a first-year English student at Ulster University Coleraine in Northern Ireland. He has been writing poetry since secondary school. He obtained 2nd place in the senior section of the Patrick Kavanagh Student Poetry Award. He is influenced by his home of Ireland, its nature and many Irish poets and writers, particularly Patrick Kavanagh, Seamus Heaney and Derek Mahon. He is also a musician and teaches beginner's guitar. He lives in County Fermanagh with his parents, his brother and his dog. He hopes to go on to work in publishing and to continue having his own writing published.

LUCA GOATEN was born in East Yorkshire in 1996 and grew up in Hull. He is a poet, writer, and student. He recently graduated from his undergraduate degree in Italian and English Literature MA at the University of Edinburgh, and he is currently reading Comparative Literature MPhil at the University of Cambridge. His poetry has been published in various poetry magazines in both English and Italian.

ANDREW GOOCH is 24 years old and has been writing and performing spoken word for the last two years in and around the Hull area. He has been part of BBC's Contains Strong Language and various local literature festivals. His work is primarily centred around the theme of anxiety and depression and how it effects young people in the modern day.

ELEN GRIFFITHS is a 30 year old poet living in London, by day a charity lawyer. This year her poems have been shortlisted for the Bridport Prize and for publication in *Magma*, and longlisted for the *Brotherton Prize*. In the past, she has been named as a Commended Poet in the *Foyle Young Poets of the Year* award.

APRIL HILL is a Chinese/British lesbian poet and writer concerned with intimacies, and has previously been published in *We Were Always Here* by Queer Words Project Scotland, *Multiverse* by Shoreline of Infinity, and the second edition of *Umbrellas of Edinburgh* by Russell Jones and Claire Askew, as well as by magazines *404 Ink* and *Zarf Poetry*.

REBECCA KANE is a 19 year old poet from a little town outside of Glasgow called Airdrie. Rebecca only started writing poetry around the start of 2019. Poetry has helped her overcome depression and body dysmorphia which are ideas and themes present within her work. Rebecca takes what she has struggled with and made it into something beautiful. Her work falls into the category of the grotesque and strange with heavy body image mixed with the whimsical.

ARUN KAPUR Enigmatic. Charismatic. Fanatic. Lover of life and all things natural. Wolverhampton born and bred. Poet, film maker, story teller. Art runs through my veins and powers my soul.

SIAN MITCHELL is a poet working in the heritage sector. Born in Coventry, she studied at the University of Birmingham and the University of Oxford, where she read nineteenth-century literature. In Oxford she developed her love of weird, wonderful and quirky historical buildings, and she has worked in heritage education at Blenheim Palace, Coventry Cathedral and Worcester Cathedral. Sian has been writing poetry for several years, and was a finalist in the Worcestershire Poet Laureate competition in 2019.

VAISHNAVI PARIHAR is a firm believer of bringing change in the society with a pen and a smile. Vaishnavi is a seventeen year old artist, book addict and an impulsive closet writer residing in India. Her poems question norms and portray naked truth, sometimes subtle, sometimes clearly evident. She loves the ocean and it's breeze as much as she loves metaphors, surrealism and the colour blue.
https://midnightbluesx.wordpress.com/

LAUREN RANSON is a poet based in Hull who, starting as a bedroom rapper, discovered poetry by attending workshops led by Toby Campion and performing at the Regional Heats of the Roundhouse Poetry Slam 2019. Since then, she has gone on to perform for BBC Introducing Humberside and at various events around the country in places such as London, Exeter, Leeds, and Halifax. She has performed at *Freedom Festival*, *Contains Strong Language* and *Engage 4 Change*, and her work has appeared in *Bonnie's Crew*. She was recently selected by Apples and Snakes to attend the *Writing Rooms* workshop series with Jacob Sam-La Rose. She is a Co-Founder of the Hull-based Young Poets Collective *No Larkin About*.

NIA WYN ROBERTS is a writer and poet who grew up in North Wales. Her Welsh roots heavily influence her poetry and her passion for language, both Welsh and English.

Niâ has a degree in Film Production, and currently lives in East Manchester. During the day she is the Senior Underwriter for a European Insurance company.

GRACE ROYAL is a recent university graduate who writes both poetry and prose. Her work focuses on the everyday, the small details of life and the presence of the internet and social media in the contemporary world. She likes to experiment with form while also drawing inspiration from classic literature. Grace has completed an undergraduate degree in English and Creative Writing and a Masters in English Literature at Royal Holloway.

NATASHA RUBINS is a London based poet. A recent graduate of English Literature currently working in the charity sector, her personal achievements include playing a wardrobe in a school play.

HESTER ULLYART was born in Hull and educated at Wyke College and the Royal Academy of Dramatic Art. With a background in the Hull and London alternative music scene (The City Ghosts, Night Flowers) and professional theatre, she is now developing her own voice through the writing and performance of original plays, prose and poetry.

She performed her debut play The Ballad of Paragon Station in London, Edinburgh, Hull and New Zealand in 2017 and 2018, soon followed by Paragon Dreams (Hull Truck 2019). A national tour of Paragon Dreams is scheduled for 2020.

More about Hester can be found at www.hesterullyart.com

www.ingramcontent.com/pod-product-compliance
Lightning Source LLC
Chambersburg PA
CBHW011316080526
44587CB00024B/4013